A Literature Kit™ FOR

The Great Gilly Hopkins

By Katherine Paterson

Written by Marie-Helen Goyetche

GRADES 5 - 6

Classroom Complete Press
P.O. Box 19729
San Diego, CA 92159
Tel: 1-800-663-3609 / Fax: 1-800-663-3608
Email: service@classroomcompletepress.com

www.classroomcompletepress.com

ISBN-13: 978-1-55319-336-4
ISBN-10: 1-55319-336-9

© 2007

Critical Thinking Skills

The Great Gilly Hopkins

Skills For Critical Thinking	Chapter Questions										Writing Tasks	Graphic Organizers
	1	2	3	4	5	6-7	8-9	10-11	12-13	14-15		
LEVEL 1 Knowledge												
• Identify Story Elements				✓			✓		✓			✓
• Recall Details	✓	✓	✓	✓	✓	✓	✓	✓	✓	✓	✓	✓
• Match	✓	✓	✓		✓	✓	✓	✓		✓		
• Sequence	✓		✓				✓			✓		✓
LEVEL 2 Comprehension												
• Compare Characters	✓			✓		✓	✓				✓	✓
• Summarize		✓		✓	✓	✓	✓		✓	✓		✓
• State Main Idea		✓			✓	✓	✓				✓	✓
• Describe	✓			✓		✓	✓					✓
• Classify									✓			✓
LEVEL 3 Application												
• Plan	✓	✓	✓	✓	✓		✓	✓		✓		
• Interview							✓		✓	✓	✓	✓
• Make Inferences	✓	✓	✓	✓	✓	✓	✓					
LEVEL 4 Analysis												
• Draw Conclusions	✓	✓	✓	✓	✓	✓	✓		✓	✓		✓
• Identify Supporting Evidence	✓	✓	✓				✓					✓
• Infer Character Motivations	✓	✓	✓	✓	✓				✓	✓		✓
• Identify Cause & Effect			✓		✓	✓			✓	✓		✓
LEVEL 5 Synthesis												
• Predict	✓	✓	✓	✓	✓	✓	✓	✓	✓	✓		
• Design (i.e., An Invitation)											✓	
• Create					✓	✓					✓	
• Imagine Alternatives										✓	✓	
LEVEL 6 Evaluation												
• Defend An Opinion	✓	✓	✓	✓	✓	✓	✓	✓	✓	✓	✓	
• Make Judgements			✓		✓	✓	✓			✓		

Based on Bloom's Taxonomy

Contents

✔ **6 BONUS** Activity Pages! **Additional worksheets for your students**
✔ **3 BONUS** Overhead Transparencies! **For use with your projection system**

FREE!

- Go to our website: **www.classroomcompletepress.com\bonus**
- Enter item CC2504 or The Great Gilly Hopkins
- Enter pass code CC2504D for Activity Pages. CC2504A for Overheads.

Assessment Rubric

The Great Gilly Hopkins

Student's Name: _____   Assignment: _____   Level: _____

SKILLS/KNOWLEDGE	Level 1	Level 2	Level 3	Level 4
Comprehension of the Novel	Demonstrates a limited understanding of the novel	Demonstrates a basic understanding of the novel	Demonstrates a good understanding of the novel	Demonstrates a thorough understanding of the novel
Content	Information incomplete; key details missing	Some information complete; details missing	All required information complete; key details contain some description	All required information complete; enough description for clarity
Style	Little variety in word choice; language vague and imprecise	Some variety in word choice; language somewhat vague and imprecise	Good variety in word choice; language precise and quite descriptive	Writer's voice is apparent throughout. Excellent choice of words; precise language.
Conventions	Errors seriously interfere with the writer's purpose	Repeated errors in mechanics and usage	Some errors in convention	Few errors in convention

STRENGTHS:

WEAKNESSES:

NEXT STEPS:

Teacher Guide

Our resource has been created for ease of use by both TEACHERS and STUDENTS alike.

Introduction

The Great Gilly Hopkins is one of several award-winning novels written by Katherine Paterson, and has proven to be tremendously popular with young people. Recognized as a Newbery Honor Book, this is the highly entertaining story of a bold and brazen eleven-year-old girl – and foster child – who has great expectations about life; she dreams of finding her mother and living with her again. Over the course of the novel, Gilly learns many valuable lessons about family, friendship, and what it means to be loved by those around her.

How Is This Literature Kit™ Organized?

STUDENT HANDOUTS
Chapter Activities (in the form of reproducible worksheets) make up the majority of this resource. For each chapter or group of chapters there are BEFORE YOU READ activities and AFTER YOU READ activities.

- The BEFORE YOU READ activities prepare students for reading by setting a purpose for reading. They stimulate background knowledge and experience, and guide students to make connections between what they know and what they will learn. Important concepts and vocabulary from the chapter(s) are also presented.

- The AFTER YOU READ activities check students' comprehension and extend their learning. Students are asked to give thoughtful consideration of the text through creative and evaluative short-answer questions and journal prompts.

Six **Writing Tasks** and three **Graphic Organizers** are included to further develop students' critical thinking and writing skills, and analysis of the text. (See page 6 for suggestions on using the Graphic Organizers.) The **Assessment Rubric** (page 4) is a useful tool for evaluating students' responses to the Writing Tasks and Graphic Organizers.

PICTURE CUES
This resource contains three main types of pages, each with a different purpose and use. A **Picture Cue** at the top of each page shows, at a glance, what the page is for.

 Teacher Guide
- Information and tools for the teacher

 Student Handout
- Reproducible worksheets and activities

 Easy Marking™ Answer Key
- Answers for student activities

EASY MARKING™ ANSWER KEY
Marking students' worksheets is fast and easy with this **Answer Key**. Answers are listed in columns – just line up the column with its corresponding worksheet, as shown, and see how every question matches up with its answer!

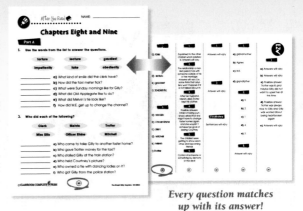

Every question matches up with its answer!

1,2,3
Graphic Organizer Transparencies

The three **Graphic Organizer Transparencies** included in this Literature Kit™ are especially suited to a study of *The Great Gilly Hopkins*. Below are suggestions for using each organizer in your classroom, or they may be adapted to suit the individual needs of your students. The transparencies can be used on an overhead projector in teacher-led activities, and/or photocopied for use as student worksheets.
To evaluate students' responses to any of the organizers, you may wish to use the **Assessment Rubric** (*on page 4*).

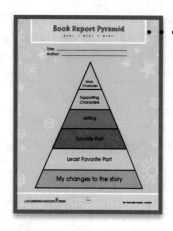

BOOK REPORT TRIANGLE

This Organizer may be used as an alternative to the traditional book report, or it may be used to plan a book report. Students record the title and author of the book, and complete the triangle with information on key story elements: main character, supporting characters, and setting (where and when the story takes place). They are to describe their favorite and least favorite parts of the novel, giving good reasons for their choices, and then indicate the changes they would make to the story to improve upon it, again giving good reasons as to why their changes would improve the story. Found on Page 53.

SURVEY ORGANIZER

For this activity students conduct an informal survey. Students begin by brainstorming a list of everything they consider important in their daily lives (i.e., having friends, feeling loved, etc.) and recording the ten most important items in the chart. Then, they survey five other students, the teacher and themselves, asking if each item is important in their daily lives. For "Yes", put a check mark in the box, for "No", leave it blank. Students are to infer what Gilly and W.E. would answer. Lastly, have students create four questions based on their survey findings and exchange their questions with a partner. Found on Page 54.

GILLY'S FOSTER FAMILIES

This Graphic Organizer is a useful tool to help students identify the six different families Gilly lived with as a foster child, and her responses to each family. In the left hand column, students are to write down the name of each foster family in the correct chronological order. In the second column, have students record as many significant details as they can about the time Gilly spent with each family (examples include: What happened while Gilly lived with this family? How did she feel about living with this family? How long did she stay? What were the reasons for her leaving?) Found on Page 55.

Bloom's Taxonomy* for Reading Comprehension

The activities in this resource engage and build the full range of thinking skills that are essential for students' reading comprehension. Based on the six levels of thinking in Bloom's Taxonomy, questions are given that challenge students to not only recall what they have read, but move beyond this to understand the text through higher-order thinking. By using higher-order skills of application, analysis, synthesis and evaluation, students become active readers, drawing more meaning from the text, and applying and extending their learning in more sophisticated ways.

This Literature Kit™, therefore, is an effective tool for any Language Arts program. Whether it is used in whole or in part, or adapted to meet individual student needs, this resource provides teachers with the important questions to ask, inspiring students' interest, creativity, and promoting meaningful learning.

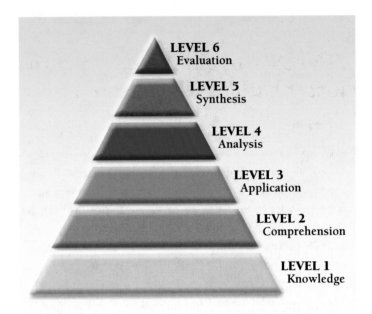

BLOOM'S TAXONOMY:
6 LEVELS OF THINKING

*Bloom's Taxonomy is a widely used tool by educators for classifying learning objectives, and is based on the work of Benjamin Bloom.

Teaching Strategies — WHOLE-CLASS, SMALL GROUP AND INDEPENDENT STUDY

The Great Gilly Hopkins is a novel that may be approached in several ways. Most obvious is as a traditional, whole-class read-aloud in which the teacher reads the book out loud to the entire class, stopping after one or more chapters for the students to answer the chapter questions. As they complete the questions, students reread the chapter(s) on their own. Depending on the interests and needs of your students, you may choose to apply some shared or modeled reading, focusing discussion on the author's skills, choices made in writing, and the elements of the narrative. The BEFORE YOU READ and AFTER YOU READ activities in this Literature Kit™ provide a basis for such discussions.

To facilitate small group and independent study learning, these activities have been divided into chapter groupings to allow students to work on manageable sections of the novel, and not feel overwhelmed by the activities. Teachers may also choose to use only a selection of the activities in this resource for small group or independent study, assigning tasks that match students' specific needs, and allowing students to work at their own speed. The components of this resource make it flexible and easy to adapt as not all of the activities need to be completed.

Teachers may wish to have their students keep a daily reading log so that they might record their daily progress and reflections. Journaling prompts have been included at the end of each chapter section to facilitate students' thinking and writing.

Summary of the Story

A STORY about a bold and brazen eleven-year-old girl – and foster child – who has great expectations about life.

T*he Great Gilly Hopkins is a highly entertaining story of a bold and brazen eleven-year-old girl named Galadriel (Gilly for short) who has great expectations about life. As the novel begins Gilly moves into her fifth foster home, the house of Maime Trotter, in fewer than three years. There she meets several interestesting characters including seven-year-old William Ernest, who is in Gilly's mind, just "freaky", and Maime's African-American neighbor, Mr. Randloph. Living with the Trotters for any length of time, however, is the last thing Gilly wants to do. Having been in foster care since she was an infant, she dreams of finding her real mother, Courtney, and living with her again.*

Gilly eventually finds Courtney's address and secretly writes a letter to her describing, with much exaggeration, her life and circumstances with the Trotters. Gilly is both hopeful that her mother will rescue her, and ready to try anything to escape – the only thing she needs is money. To solve her dilemma, Gilly steals money from Mr. Randolph and Trotter, and then heads to the bus station to buy a ticket to San Francisco. The ticket clerk, however, stops Gilly in her tracks, calls the police, and in the end, Maime takes Gilly back home.

Much to her surprise, Gilly begins to adjust to life with the Trotters. Then, on Thanksgiving weekend, when Gilly is busy taking care of everyone because they are sick with the stomach flu, Courtney's mother (Gilly's grandmother) shows up. She has come to take Gilly to live with her in Virginia. Once again, Gilly must move to a new home against her will. This move however, will be permanent. Gilly is upset because she realizes how comfortable she is and how loved she feels at the Trotter's house.

Over the course of the novel, Gilly learns many valuable lessons about life, relationships and prejudices. She comes to understand the importance of family, friendships, and what it means to be loved by those around her.

Suggestions for Further Reading

BOOKS BY KATHERINE PATERSON
The Sign of the Chrysanthemum © 1973
Of Nightingales That Weep © 1974
The Master Puppeteer © 1976
Bridge to Terabithia © 1977
Jacob Have I Loved © 1980
Rebels of the Heavenly Kingdom © 1983
Come Sing, Jimmy Jo © 1985
Park's Quest © 1988
Lyddie © 1991
Flip-Flop Girl © 1994
Jip, His Story © © 1996
Preacher's Boy © 1999
The Same Stuff as Stars © 2002

OTHER RECOMMENDED RESOURCES
Lois Lowry, *Number the Stars* © 1989
Jerry Spinelli, *Maniac Magee* © 1990
Louis Sachar, *Holes* © 1998
Christopher Paul Curtis, *Bud, Not Buddy* © 1999

Vocabulary

CHAPTERS 1 AND 2
• cautious • elaborately • professional • bolster • satisfaction • gruesome • caseworker • repertory • barracuda • flinch • laboriously • maneuver • obligingly • prodding • salvage • squat • straggly

CHAPTERS 3 TO 5
• astray • acquaintance • bowel • curlicue • cuss • delinquency • fanatic • flattery • incedent • lurch • luxuries • mock • necessity • polecat • privilege • self-righteous • vengeance

CHAPTERS 6 AND 7
• assault • bulldozed • clamor • condemned • craned • departmentalization • emphatically • evaporated • favoritism • fracas • halfheartedly • ignorant • imbecile • lard • leastways • meekly • menacing • mercilessly • obscenity • palsy • peculiar • rebound • rummaged • sassily • snarl • submission • trifle • vicious

CHAPTERS 8 TO 10
• blissfully • conspirator • divert • fret • geasily • genius • gruesome • guru • humility • lowliness • meddle • murmuring • ogre • piously • primly • shriveled • strangled • squat • vacant

CHAPTER 11
• audible • azalea • benign • clambered • delectable • enthralled • exaggerate • fledgling • halt • impulse • infuriating • interpret • leering • louse • lilt • obviously • socket • solemnly • tentative • threshold • ventured • withered

CHAPTERS 12 TO 14
• anonymous • anticipation • anxiety • aptitude • cajoling • courted • cursed • despised • despite • encase • garment • impersonal • tamperproof • vested • bribery • delinquent • marrow • merit • painstakingly • psychologist • rickety • stoke • strain

CHAPTERS 15 TO 17
• adultery • anointed • botched • dignity • eternal • exquisite • fanatic • steadfastly • flirtation • futile • gaudiest • pirouetting • preservation • reluctant • tutus • commotion • demon • engulf • hoarse • indication • possession

CHAPTERS 18 TO 20
• annoyance • appalling • apparition • burlap • cascading • coaxed • faltering • goddess • hoisted • hysterical • inexorably • irritability • naval • old-fashioned • pediatrician • perpetual • reclaim • relentless • supreme • teeter • unison • vain • kaleidoscopic • tittered

CHAPTERS 21 TO 23
• disguise • belligerently • smoochers • canopied • monogrammed • elaborately • straddle • drowsiness • commendation • crankiness • expanse • expression • hightailed • indefinitely • merriment • pervades • permanence • reputation • rhythmic • squawking • ultimate • woefully

CHAPTERS 24 TO 26
• agony • prissy • lopsided • tattered • appalling • chatter • dulled • gutsy • plunging • sneer • anxiety • perspiration • homecoming • impatient • permanent • reckon • willowy • gorgeous • timid • embroidered

Katherine Paterson

K atherine Paterson was born in Qing Jiang, Jiangsu, China in 1932. Her parents were American missionaries working in China. As she was growing up she learned the Chinese language, and how to respect differences between people. By the time she was eighteen years old, she had moved eighteen times. She felt terribly lonely and found refuge in books.

Back in the United States, Katherine graduated from King College in Bristol, Tennessee with an English degree. She worked in a small rural school in Virginia for a year before returning to school in Richmond, Virginia. Like her parents, she had wanted to become a missionary in China, but in the late 1950's China was not allowing any Americans into their country. She decided to go to Japan instead where she lived for four years.

By 1962, Katherine had returned to the United States, and her life as a writer began. She began writing nonfiction books, and in the process, realized that what she really wanted to write was fiction. Then, after taking a creative writing class for adults she wrote and published her first work of fiction, The Sign of the Chrysanthemum in 1973.

Katherine has always loved reading fiction. She believed it was important for children to read fiction and connect with the real world through stories. Katherine creates realistic characters

that young people can relate to. Her characters have real life experiences, and by reading about them, young people can learn important lessons about life and the world in which they live. It was Katherine's experiences of being a foster mother herself that inspired her to write The Great Gilly Hopkins. She didn't think that she was a good foster parent and decided to write something from the point of view of a foster child. Looking back, Katherine feels that her experiences in China and Japan, and her strong Biblical heritage all contributed to the tone, ideas and themes in her books.

Did You Know?

- When she was growing up Katherine wanted to be a movie star.
- Katherine's hobbies include playing the piano and tennis.
- The Great Gilly Hopkins won the Newbery Honor Award and 5 other awards

Chapter One

Answer the questions in complete sentences.

1. Katherine Paterson is the author of The Great Gilly Hopkins. She also wrote Park's Quest, Jip, His Story, Jacob Have I Loved and Bridge to Terabithia (just to name a few). How familiar are you with this author? Why do you think her books are so appealing to young teens?

   _____

   _____

2. Before you begin the novel, look at the front cover. What does the image show? What kind of character do you think Gilly Hopkins is?

   _____

   _____

Vocabulary

Write each word beside its definition. Then, use each word in a sentence that shows its meaning.

bolster   obligingly   flinch   prodding

salvage   squat

1. In an accommodating manner

2. Poking with something pointy

3. To save something from danger

4. To sit down upon one's heels

5. To shrink or drawback

6. A long pillow

Chapter One

Part A

1. **Circle** **T** if the statement is **TRUE** or **F** if it is **FALSE.**

   T   F   **a)** This is Gilly's second foster home.

   T   F   **b)** Miss Ellis is Gilly's social worker.

   T   F   **c)** Gilly gave W.E. the most fearful face in all her repertory.

   T   F   **d)** Gilly blew her bubble gum into a bubble right into Miss Ellis' hair.

   T   F   **e)** Gilly's real name is Galadriel Hopkins.

   T   F   **f)** Gilly had perfected how to vomit at will.

2. **Number the events from ❶ to ❻ in the order they occurred in the chapter.**

   _____ **a)** Miss Ellis prodded Gilly through the doorway.

   _____ **b)** Mrs. Trotter opened the door and welcomed them to Thompson Park.

   _____ **c)** Gilly was going for the Guinness Record for uncombed hair.

   _____ **d)** Miss Ellis told Gilly the change of address was not her fault.

   _____ **e)** Gilly smiled at Miss Ellis.

   _____ **f)** Gilly gave William a look.

NAME: _____

Chapter One

Part B

Answer the questions in complete sentences.

1. How do you think Gilly felt being sent to yet another foster home?

   _____

   _____

2. How long do you think Gilly will stay at Mrs. Trotter's? Predict the length of time in months.

   _____

   _____

3. Why do you think Gilly gave William such a fearful look?

   _____

   _____

4. If you were Gilly, how would you get Mrs. Trotter to like you?

   _____

   _____

5. What do you suppose happened to Gilly's parents?

   _____

   _____

6. Would you like your familiy to be a foster family? Why or why not?

   _____

   _____

Journal Prompt

Imagine that you are another foster child living with William Ernest and Mrs. Trotter. You want to help Gilly, the new foster child, feel comfortable. What will you do to accomplish this? Describe your plans in detail. How important do you think it is for Gilly to feel welcomed?

 Before You Read   NAME: _____

Chapter Two

Answer the questions in complete sentences.

1. What do you predict will happen between Gilly and William Ernest?

_____

_____

2. Do you know anyone, or have you ever met someone who has a physical disability? Briefly describe an interaction you had with this person, either the time you first met, or another interaction you had together.

_____

_____

Vocabulary

Write each word next to its synonym or pair of synonyms. (Remember: synonyms are different words that have the same, or similar meanings.) Use a dictionary to help you.

acquaintance	curlicue	delinquency	fanatic
lurch	polecat	privilege	vengeance

1. perogative, right   _____

2. coil, twist   _____

3. maniac, enthusiast   _____

4. friend   _____

5. weasel   _____

6. falter, stagger   _____

7. retaliation, retribution   _____

8. default, failure   _____

After You Read 📖

Chapter Two

Part A

1. Put a check mark next to the answer that is most correct.

a) Who went to get Mr. Randolph at suppertime?
- ○ **A** William Ernest
- ○ **B** Gilly
- ○ **C** Trotter

b) What was Gilly's mother name?
- ○ **A** Courtney Robertson Hopkins
- ○ **B** Courtney Robinson Hopkins
- ○ **C** Courtney Rutherford Hopkins

c) Courtney was from which state?
- ○ **A** Alabama
- ○ **B** Virginia
- ○ **C** Florida

d) William Ernest watched which television show?
- ○ **A** Sesame Street
- ○ **B** Zoom
- ○ **C** Captain Kangaroo

2. Put a check mark next to the answer that is most correct.

a) How Gilly felt when she heard the word "mother"?
- ○ **A** Like Jell-O
- ○ **B** Like ketchup
- ○ **C** Like putty

b) Trotter's response when she thought Gilly called W.E. a "retard"?
- ○ **A** Offensive, to protect Gilly
- ○ **B** Mad, to protect Miss Ellis
- ○ **C** Defensive, to protect W.E.

c) What Gilly did when she saw Mr. Randolph?
- ○ **A** Ran into the kitchen
- ○ **B** Hugged him
- ○ **C** Sat down with him for coffee

d) W.E., during supper time?
- ○ **A** Wouldn't stop talking
- ○ **B** Wouldn't stop laughing
- ○ **C** Silent and steady

NAME: _____

Chapter Two

Part B

Answer the questions in complete sentences.

1. Do you think Mrs. Trotter is wealthy? Explain.

   _____

   _____

2. If you were a character in this novel and Gilly told you she had never touched a colored person before, how would you respond? What would you say to her?

   _____

   _____

3. From what we know about Gilly so far, she seems mean and tough. Yet she caught Mr. Randolph and stopped him from falling on his face. Why do you suppose she did this?

   _____

   _____

4. What lies do you think Miss Ellis told Gilly? Why do you think she did this?

   _____

   _____

5. A **simile** is a literary device two different things are compared using the words like or as. For example, in Chapter Two, Gilly realizes that **"it was not the time to start dissolving like hot Jell-O"**. The author uses a simile to compare Gilly's feelings to the dissolving of hot Jell-O. Try to find three more similes in the chapter.

   _____

   _____

Journal Prompt

Imagine that you are Gilly's friend and you have just learned where Courtney lives. Write a letter to Courtney telling her about her daughter. Tell her how Gilly feels, and describe the fears and concerns she has because they are not together.

Chapter Three

• •

Answer the questions in complete sentences.

1. Chapter Three is entitled, **_More Unpleasant Surprises_**. What do you think the unpleasant surprises will be?

_____

_____

2. Do you think Mr. Randolph has much of a chance of getting to know Gilly? What good could a blind man bring to an eleven-year-old girl?

_____

_____

Vocabulary

Complete each sentence with a word from the list.

clamor	vicious	favoritism	fracas	imbecile

obscene	snarled	sassy	palsy

1. The angry dog [_____] and looked [_____] .

2. He looked like such a fool; he looked like an [_____] .

3. The audience cheered so loudly they caused quite a [_____] .

4. Grandma loves all her grandchildren equally; she never shows any [_____] .

5. A person with [_____] has muscle paralysis in some or all of their body .

6. I know they were arguing because of the [_____] .

7. A lot of [_____] words came out of Gilly's mouth .

8. Gilly was very disrespectful and [_____] toward Trotter .

NAME: _____

Chapter Three

Part A

1. (Circle) **T** if the statement is TRUE or **F** if it is FALSE.

T F **a)** William Ernest wiped Trotter's nose.

T F **b)** Miss Ellis showed favoritism toward William Ernest over Gilly.

T F **c)** Mr. Evans, the principal, greeted Gilly.

T F **d)** Mr. Evans believes that Gilly should be in a challenging class.

T F **e)** Gilly was placed in a regular grade six class.

T F **f)** Gilly compared school to a prison.

2. **Read the following statements. Put an X on the line to indicate how much you AGREE or DISAGREE with each. Justify your decisions in the space provided. Compare and discuss your opinions with a partner.**

a) It is okay for a student who is new at school to do whatever it takes to get respect.

Agree ------------------------------------- Disagree

Justification:

b) All students who fight should be suspended.

Agree ------------------------------------- Disagree

Justification:

Chapter Three

Part B

Answer the questions in complete sentences.

1. Gilly and W.E. are both foster children, yet Gilly is very mean to W.E.. Why do you think she is so mean to him?

_____

_____

2. Have you ever changed schools? How did you feel? How do you think you would react?

_____

_____

3 a) What went wrong at recess with Gilly and the boys? Do you think she got into a fight with six boys on purpose?

_____

_____

b) In your opinion, what should the consequences be for her actions?

_____

_____

4. A metaphor is a comparison of two things in which one thing is described as being something completely unrelated. For example, in Chapter Three, the author writes, "From the doorway (Gilly) could hear Old Mother Goose honking over her gosling". Find one more example of a metaphor in this chapter.

_____

_____

Journal Prompt

Reread the section of Chapter Three in which Miss Harris is introduced to Gilly. Then, write an alternative scenario describing how things could have happened differently. Perhaps Miss Harris and Gilly know each from another school. Maybe they argue when they first meet. Be creative!

NAME: _____

Chapter Four

Answer the questions in complete sentences.

1. Do you think Gilly will give her new school a chance? Do you think she will give her-self a chance?

    _____

    _____

2. In the last chapter Gilly got into a fight with six boys. Was this an effective way of gaining their respect? How might she be able to get their respect now? Do you think she will be respected by the girls?

    _____

    _____

    _____

Vocabulary

Use a dictionary to find the definitions of the words below. Write each word in a sentence that shows the meaning of the word.

1. **piously** _____

2. **fret** _____

3. **guru** _____

4. **conspirator** _____

5. **swat** _____

6. **divert** _____

After You Read 📖

Chapter Four

Part A

1. **Use the words in the list to answer the questions.**

(ticket)   (postcard)   (two five-dollar bills)   (Bible)

(Bible)   (encyclopedia)   (root)

_____ **a)** Which book did Trotter and Mr. Randolph want Gilly to read?

_____ **b)** What did Gilly find at Mr. Randolph's house?

_____ **c)** What is Sarsaparilla?

_____ **d)** What did Gilly get from Courtney?

_____ **e)** What type of book was Sarsaparilla to Sorcery?

_____ **f)** What would Gilly buy with the money?

2. **Number the events from ❶ to ❻ in the order they occurred in Chapters One to Four.**

_____ **a)** Galadriel received a letter from Courtney.

_____ **b)** Gilly read poems to Mr. Randolph.

_____ **c)** Gilly was afraid she would have to read the Bible.

_____ **d)** Gilly scared W.E. so much he choked on a carrot.

_____ **e)** Gilly found two five-dollar bills behind the book on the shelf.

_____ **f)** Gilly was invited over to Agnes' house, but she didn't want to go.

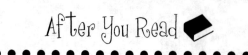

NAME: _____

Chapter Four

Part B

Answer each question with a complete sentence.

1. Why do you think Mr. Randolph hid his money? Do you think there will be more? What would you have done, if you had found the two five-dollar bills?

   _____

   _____

2. If you had an opportunity to read to an elderly person, what books would you like to share with them? Would you prefer reading to an elderly person or a very young child? Explain.

   _____

   _____

3. Why do you think no one had ever noticed the money on the shelf?

   _____

   _____

4. How could you convince Gilly that W.E. is a good boy?

   _____

   _____

5. In Chapter Four Trotter says, "One man's trash is another man's treasure". Explain what this statement means in your own words.

   _____

   _____

Journal Prompt

Sarsaparilla to Sorcery is the encyclopedia in which Gilly found the money. List as many words as you can that might be found alphabetically in this encyclopedia, between the words "Sarsaparilla" and "Sorcery". For example: "<u>sauce</u>" might appear between these words, but "sandwich" would not, since alphabetically, "<u>sandwich</u>" would be listed before "<u>Sarsaparilla</u>".

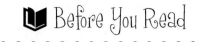

Chapter Five

Answer the questions in complete sentences.

1. Do you think Gilly will go back to Mr. Randolph's to see if there's more money? If you were Gilly, what would you do?

_____

_____

2. Is Gilly realistic in thinking that she can get a one-way ticket back to her mom? What important point can you think of that Gilly hasn't considered?

_____

_____

Vocabulary

Write each word beside its antonym. (Remember: antonyms are words that have opposite meanings.) Then, for each pair of antonyms, write a sentence that includes both words within the same sentence.

distasteful   distant   misunderstand   obscure

proceed   final

1. **tentative**

2. **delectable**

3. **immediate**

4. **halt**

5. **obvious**

6. **interpret**

Chapter Five

Part A

1. **Put a check mark next to the answer that is most correct.**

    a) What did Gilly accuse Agnes of having?

    ○ **A** A big nose
    ○ **B** Big red hair
    ○ **C** A big mouth

    b) Who did Gilly decide to use to help her in her life of crime?

    ○ **A** Agnes Stokes
    ○ **B** Mr. Randolph
    ○ **C** William Ernest

    c) Gilly and W.E. watched which television shows together?

    ○ **A** Sesame Street, Mr. Roger's Neighborhood and Zoom
    ○ **B** Mr. Roger's Neighborhood, The Electric Company and Captain Kangaroo
    ○ **C** The Electric Company, Sesame Street and Mr. Roger's Neighborhood

    d) What did Gilly do for W.E.?

    ○ **A** She built him a model airplane.
    ○ **B** She built him a paper airplane.
    ○ **C** She gave him two five-dollar bills.

2. **Which answer best describes:**

    a) How Trotter would feel if Gilly was too nice to W.E.?

    ○ **A** suspicious
    ○ **B** angry
    ○ **C** over emotional

    b) What Gilly did to make Trotter's heart melt?

    ○ **A** She faked a smile.
    ○ **B** She cried.
    ○ **C** She laughed her head off.

    c) W.E., as he climbed up the concrete post?

    ○ **A** over confident
    ○ **B** strong
    ○ **C** afraid

    d) How Trotter felt when he saw W.E. flying his plane?

    ○ **A** mad
    ○ **B** thankful
    ○ **C** nostalgic

After You Read 📖

Chapter Five

Part B

Answer each question with a complete sentence.

1. Do you think using people to get what you want is an acceptable thing to do?

_____

_____

2. Why was Gilly upset that Trotter made chocolate chip cookies?

_____

_____

3. Write down some advice for Agnes that would help her be more assertive.

_____

_____

4. Do you think Mr. Randolph sees through Gilly and her personality?

_____

_____

5. **Onomatopoeia** is the use of words that imitate the sounds of the actions or objects they represent. The words **buzz, kerplunk** and **splash** are good examples of onomatopoeia. Look through Chapter Five and write down all the examples of onomatopoeia that you can find.

_____

_____

Journal Prompt

Agnes Stokes is a special little girl and an interesting character in the novel. Write a Character Description of Agnes. Create a chart and fill in important details about her appearance, feelings and emotions, and thoughts and behaviors. Would you want to have Agnes as a friend? Why or why not?

Chapters Six and Seven

Answer the questions in complete sentences.

1. What was Gilly's plan? Why do you think she did not include Trotter in her plan?

_____

_____

2. Think about all of the teachers you have had. Which one did you enjoy the most? With whom did you learn the most? Give good reasons for your answers.

_____

_____

_____

_____

Vocabulary

Complete the chart by adding the correct word for each definition. Then, write down each word's part of speech. Use a dictionary to help you.

aptitude   marrow   cajole   courted

stoke   anonymous

Word	Definition	Part of speech
	Fatty substance found within bones	
	Capacity	
	Tried to attract, win over, or woo	
	Nameless	
	To feed or tend to a fire	
	To persuade gently with flattery	

Chapters Six and Seven

Part A

1. **Circle** **T** if the statement is **TRUE** or **F** if it is **FALSE**.

T　F　**a)** As if he had never left, Agnes' father was still listed in the phone book.

T　F　**b)** At her old school, they sent for the army to come and figure her out.

T　F　**c)** Gilly had to pay W.E. and Agnes to stay quiet.

T　F　**d)** Gilly borrowed money from Mr. Randolph so she could buy "school supplies".

T　F　**e)** Gilly had the guts to call her mother, Courtney, to tell her how miserable she was.

T　F　**f)** Miss Harris was so upset about her card, she quit her job.

2. **Who said each of the following? (One name is used more than once.)**

Gilly　　Miss Harris　　Mr. Randolph

Agnes　　Trotter

_____ **a)** "Dust? I guess not."

_____ **b)** "There's no danger of that, Mrs. Trotter."

_____ **c)** "Gilly, but you and I are very much alike."

_____ **d)** "You're the doctor, Miss Gilly."

_____ **e)** "If it wasn't for me, you'd be caught right now."

_____ **f)** "I-I-I'm sort of straightening up the book shelves."

Chapters Six and Seven

Part B

Answer each question with a complete sentence.

1. In Gilly's letter to her mother, what did Gilly say about her circumstances? What did she say about Trotter, W.E. and Mr. Randolph? How did you feel when you read the letter?

   _____

   _____

2. How much money is Gilly missing now? Where do you think she will be able to get that amount of money?

   _____

   _____

3. How long do you think Mr. Randolph had his money hidden away? Do you think he forgot about it, or is he testing Gilly?

   _____

   _____

4. Do you think that Gilly should keep the money? If you do, write one or two supporting sentences that show your approval. If you disagree, write one or two sentences that convey your disapproval.

   _____

   _____

5. If they get caught, what consequences should there be? Should the consequences be the same for all of them?

   _____

   _____

Journal Prompt

> **Gilly made a special card for Miss Harris. Instead of receiving it negatively, Miss Harris took the message in a positive light and thanked Gilly for her card. Do the opposite of Gilly – create a card for one of your favorite teachers. If this is not for your present teacher, ask how the card could be sent to the other teacher if he or she is in another school.**

 Before You Read

Chapters Eight and Nine

Answer the questions in complete sentences.

1. How do you think Courtney will react to the letter from Gilly?

_____

_____

2. Have you ever attended Sunday School, or another kind of school or class for religious reasons? What was most memorable about your experience?

_____

_____

Vocabulary

Write each word next to its synonyms.

dignity	eternal	exquisite	futile
indication	pirouetting	preservation	reluctant

1. **infinite, endless, perpetual**

2. **ineffective, useless, unsuccessful**

3. **spinning, whirling, twirling**

4. **disinclined, afraid, averse**

5. **expression, gesture, sign**

6. **protection, safeguard, defense**

7. **elegant, superior, dainty**

8. **honor, prestige, respect**

NAME: _____

Chapters Eight and Nine

Part A

1. **Use the words from the list to answer the questions.**

torture   lecture   gaudiest

impatiently   fake   obediently

_____ **a)** What kind of smile did the clerk have?

_____ **b)** How did the taxi meter tick?

_____ **c)** What were Sunday mornings like for Gilly?

_____ **d)** What did Old Applegate like to do?

_____ **e)** What did Melvin's tie look like?

_____ **f)** How did W.E. get up to change the channel?

2. **Who did each of the following?**

Clerk   Melvin   Trotter

Miss Ellis   Officer Rhine   Mitchell

_____ **a)** Who came to take Gilly to another foster home?

_____ **b)** Who gave Trotter money for the taxi?

_____ **c)** Who stalled Gilly at the train station?

_____ **d)** Who held Courtney's picture?

_____ **e)** Who owned a tie with dancing ladies on it?

_____ **f)** Who got Gilly from the police station?

Chapters Eight and Nine

Part B

Answer each question with a complete sentence.

1. How did Gilly earn 78 cents? What do you think about how she earned it?

_____

_____

2. What is **adultery?** Why do you think no one would tell the children what it was?

_____

_____

3. Why did Trotter have "man ties"?

_____

_____

4. What do you think frightened Gilly about her visit to the police station?

_____

_____

5. Why do you think Trotter began to cry when W.E. and Gilly were talking to each other?

_____

_____

6. What is meant by the expression *demon possession?*

_____

_____

Journal Prompt

Write a story using the expression "Demon Possession" as the title. Your story can be either humorous or scary. Write in a voice that you've never used before, and remember to include lots of detail.

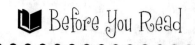
Chapters Eight and Nine

Answer the questions in complete sentences.

1. Do you think Gilly will try to escape in order to go see her mother again? What would motivate you to go, or stay?

_____

_____

2. Do you think William Ernest will use his new fighting skills? When and how will he be ready?

_____

_____

Vocabulary

Use a dictionary to find the definitions of the words below. Then, write each word in a sentence that shows its meaning.

1. dread

_____

2. appalling

_____

3. unison

_____

4. vain

_____

5. commendation

_____

6. defiant

_____

Chapters Ten and Eleven

Part A

1. **Use the words listed below to answer each question**

(**Agnes**)   (**grandfather**)   (**W.E.**)   (**grandmother**)

_____ **a)** Who was at the door?

_____ **b)** Who did Gilly expect at the door?

_____ **c)** Who was wet?

_____ **d)** Who died 12 years ago?

2. **Number the events from ❶ to ❻ in the order they occurred in the chapters.**

_____ **a)** Agnes showed up.

_____ **b)** Her grandmother showed up.

_____ **c)** Mr. Randolph showed up sick.

_____ **d)** Trotter showed up looking for the turkey.

_____ **e)** W.E. showed up with wet long johns.

3. **Read the following statement. Put an X on the line to indicate how much you AGREE or DISAGREE with it. Justify your decision in the space provided. Compare and discuss your opinion with a partner.**

Children should not have any say in where they live or with whom they live.

Agree --------------------------------- Disagree

Justification:

Chapters Ten and Eleven

Part B

1. **a)** Why do you think Courtney never told her parents about Galadriel?

_____

_____

b) If you were Courtney, would you have shared that news? What would make a person not want to tell others about the arrival of a new baby?

_____

_____

2. Why didn't Gilly explain to Trotter who the visitor was? What motivated her to keep quiet?

_____

_____

3. Why was Gilly getting more and more angry with Trotter?

_____

_____

4. Where do you think the relationship between Gilly and Agnes is going? Would you call them friends? Best friends?

_____

_____

Journal Prompt

Gilly's grandmother left and Gilly stayed at Trotter's. Your task is to write two different endings to the story. Write the first ending from the grandmother's point of view. Then write the second ending from Trotter's point of view. In what ways will they be similar and different?

Chapters Twelve and Thirteen

Answer the questions in complete sentences.

1. Do you think Gilly will go with her grandmother? How will Gilly be able to leave Trotter and W.E.?

_____

_____

2. Do you think Gilly will ever meet her mom? Will she try to run away back to Trotter's?

_____

_____

Vocabulary

Complete each sentence with a word from the list.

expanse	kaleidoscopic	eyeing
monogrammed	smother	woefully

1. For Gilly, the idea of being in a foster home was ☐ .

2. Their initials are ☐ on their towels and bathrobes.

3. At their granddad's funeral, the children cried ☐ .

4. Gilly had been curious about people ☐ her.

5. An ☐ is a wild open space.

6. She held her baby so tight, I thought she'd ☐ him.

After You Read

NAME: _____

Chapters Twelve and Thirteen

Part A

1. Circle **T** if the statement is TRUE or **F** if it is FALSE.

T F **a)** Gilly wanted to bring Agnes and William Ernest with her.

T F **b)** Mr. Randolph gave her a book of poems.

T F **c)** Gilly woke up crying because she was sad to leave.

T F **d)** Gilly's grandmother believed Gilly's letter.

T F **e)** Courtney was waiting at home for her.

T F **f)** Chadwell had children of his own.

2. **Who said each of the following? (One name is used more than once.)**

Grandmother   Gilly   W.E.

Trotter   Mr. Randolph

_____ **a)** "You got horses, Gilly?"

_____ **b)** "Oh, that's lovely, lovely country, Miss Gilly. Real Virginia horse country."

_____ **c)** "Like he tore a piece off hisself and gave it to you."

_____ **d)** "You make me proud, hear?"

_____ **e)** "I lie a lot."

_____ **f)** "Would you like me to help you unpack?"

Chapters Twelve and Thirteen

Part B

Answer each question with a complete sentence.

1. Do you believe Gilly's grandmother is doing the right thing by taking her? Why or why not?

_____

_____

2. How did Chadwell die?

_____

3. Why do you think Gilly felt more comfortable in a dead man's room rather than her own mother's?

_____

_____

4. If you were Gilly, what things would you share with your 'new' grandmother?

_____

_____

5. In Chapter Twelve, the author uses the metaphor, "to be herself, to be a swan…". (Remember: a metaphor is a comparison of two different things in which one thing is described as being something completely unrelated.) In this sentence, Gilly is described as being a swan. Find at least one more metaphor in Chapters Twelve and Thirteen. Write down the chapter in which it appears.

_____

_____

Journal Prompt   **Write two character descriptions, one of Gilly's grandfather and the second of her uncle Chadwell. Then draw and label Gilly's family tree, now that she actually has a family. Add more members to her family tree if you like.**

NAME: _____

Chapters Fourteen and Fifteen

Answer the questions in complete sentences.

1. What kind of relationships might Gilly keep with the people from Trotter's. Give reasons for your answer.

_____

_____

2. Have you ever attended a family reunion? Where was it and what was most memorable about your experience? If you have never been to a family reunion, write down a few sentences describing what you think a family reunion would be like.

_____

_____

Vocabulary

Write each word next to its synonyms.

agony	anxiety	chatter	gutsy
permanent	reckon	sneer	willow

1. **consider, deem, assume**

2. **concern, unease, worry**

3. **gibber, babble, prattle**

4. **lithe, slender, supple**

5. **durable, enduring, stable**

6. **bold, courageous, audacious**

7. **anguish, misery, distress**

8. **snicker, snigger, fleer**

NAME: _____

Chapters Fourteen and Fifteen

Part A

1. (Circle) all the lies Gilly wrote in her letters to Miss Harris and William Ernest.

busy with horses	worn out	shoveling snow
hoveling manure	half-million-dollar prize	have three maids
school is terrible	highest mark in Spelling	nobody knows anything
won one race	lost three races	gained twenty pounds
will skip to ninth grade	mom is coming	
will visit her mom at Christmas		

2. **Number the events from ❶ to ❼ in the order they occurred in the chapters.**

_____ **a)** Gilly wrote to Miss Harris.

_____ **b)** Gilly got a letter from Miss Harris.

_____ **c)** Gilly wrote to W.E. again.

_____ **d)** Gilly wrote to William Ernest.

_____ **e)** Gilly received a letter from W.E.

_____ **f)** Trotter wrote a letter back to Galadriel.

_____ **g)** Gilly wrote to W.E., Mr. Randolph and Trotter.

NAME: _____

Chapters Fourteen and Fifteen

Part B

Answer each question with a complete sentence.

1. If you could ask Courtney some questions, what would you want to know?

   _____

   _____

2. Why did Trotter tell Gilly about the lies? Who was right – Gilly or Trotter?

   _____

   _____

3. Would Trotter be proud of Gilly? Why or why not?

   _____

   _____

4. Describe the tensions and emotions felt at Gilly's last supper at Trotter's, and then at Gilly's first supper with Courtney. How were the mealtimes similar? How were they different? Which one would you prefer to attend? Why?

   _____

   _____

5. Do you prefer the Gilly we met at the beginning of the novel or the one at the end? Why?

   _____

   _____

Journal Prompt

Christmas and New Year's have come and gone. It's time for Gilly to write a letter to Trotter telling her about her two days with Courtney. Imagine that you are Gilly and write the letter telling what happened. Be sure to include lots of interesting details.

Chapters 1 and 2

Gilly Hopkins gets quite a surprise when she goes next door to get Mr. Randolph for supper. Not only is Mr. Randolph a person of color, he is also blind. Gilly isn't sure how to act when she meets him for the first time because he is so different from her.

Think of all the physical senses you have (the sense of touch, taste, smell, hearing and/or sight). Now, choose one of these senses and imagine what your daily life would be like if you no longer had this sense available to you. For example, if you have good vision, how would things be different if you could not see at all?

> Using good paragraph format, write a one-page description of your daily life without this sense. Describe how you would go about your daily activities, and how you would want people to respond to you.

Chapters 3 and 4

When was the last time you looked through an encyclopedia, either on the Internet or as a hard copy book, just to discover something new? Brainstorm three topics that interest you and about which you would like to learn more. Then, find an encyclopedia at the library or online, and read what is written about those three topics.

> For this writing task, choose ONE of the three topics you read about. Think about what information was new for you. What did you learn? Write a summary paragraph explaining what you have just discovered.

Trade your summary paragraph with a friend. What did he or she learn?

Chapters 5 and 6

Gilly wants to go see Courtney by taking a Greyhound bus to San Francisco for 136 dollars one way.

> Pick a city you would like to visit. Write a paragraph explaining why you would like to visit this city. What would you do there? How long would you stay? Who would you travel with? What interests you most about this city?

Then, investigate how you could get to your chosen destination. Using the Internet, look up the website of your local bus terminal. Which bus or busses would you need to take? When does the bus depart? How long will it take to get there? Will it be on a direct route or will you have to take another bus or another method of transportation? How much will the trip cost you?

- -

Chapters 7 and 8

While Gilly was busy dusting, the background noise was the television; Walter Cronkite was saying goodnight to his viewers. In the late 1970's when Katherine Paterson wrote this novel, Walter Cronkite was a household name for many people.

Do you know who Walter Cronkite is?

> Your task is to find out as much as you can about this man. Write a one-page summary about his life and legacy. What is he best known for? What is he doing now? Where does he live?

Tip: You may be able to find information about Walter Cronkite in an encyclopedia.

Writing Task #5

Chapters 9 to 14

In Chapter Fourteen, Gilly reads a poem from The Oxford Book of English Verse that she received as a gift from Mr. Randolph. While she is not sure what the poem means, she loves the sounds in the verse.

> **Reread the poem in the middle of Chapter Fourteen, and write a personal reflection on it. Here are some questions for you to consider as you read through the poem:**

- What does it mean to you?
- How do you feel when you read it?
- What questions does it bring to mind for you? What does it make you wonder?
- What do you like most about it?

Now, continue the poem by adding a few lines of your own.

- -

Writing Task #6

Chapter 15

The Great Gilly Hopkins ends with Gilly living in her new home with her real maternal grandmother. Although it is hard for Gilly to leave Trotter, Gilly understands that her place is alongside her grandmother.

> It's time to have a family reunion. Write a list of people you would like to invite to your reunion. Write up a menu, a music list, a list of decorations and any gifts or tokens you would like to buy for your guests. Using your lists, create a budget for your party; record the approximate cost of each item you will need to buy, and calculate the total budget.

You may also wish to create an invitation card, or a huge signature card, or a reunion banner.

NAME: _____

Word Search

Find all of the words in the Word Search. Words are written horizontally, vertically, diagonally, and some are even written backwards.

bolster	irritability	kaleidoscopic	gruesome
canopy	agony	reluctant	ignorant
acquaintance	bribery	anticipation	laboriously
curlicues	defiant	cajole	tentative
dread	engulf	clamor	polecat
exquisite	fracas	delectable	vain
gutsy	homecoming	expanse	swat

```
a f e d c f a f c l a m o r v m x w
j d y d r j k u s w v q t b s a y r
q r o a e q r l y g k x u u p t i f
z e c u m l h d n d e l f e i o v n
k a u a i f k i p b e z g l h y e s
s d v c n n m g a g o f i f u x d t
h f u s b o j n r f x b i b p g f a
s e x f c l p h y u a r s a u a n c
s q p e k z o y j t e f n b n e d e
z a m l a b o r i o u s l y l t g l
n o n e l y s r h b e e o n q g e o
h a j t e s r b y k t t b m t z t p
g g v q i i e l b a t c e l e d i q
l b u z d c b o l s t e r i r m s g
y j b t o p i d n q y j s g m h i n
s f s d s s h p h k r y k n g f u a
x w v e c y j j a a e j f o a w q c
z c a j o l e u s t b o u r f a x t
p n v t p a c q u a i n t a n c e y
t y x d i h u g u d r o b n d h n w
r e l u c t a n t h b o n t w o l u
c g j x w d k b j n q t f p g l a g
q l z o v p s s r e v i t a t n e t
```

NAME: _____

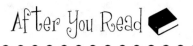
After You Read

Comprehension Quiz

Answer the questions in complete sentences.

1. Name the members of the Trotter family. Name the members of the Hopkins family

_____
_____ ②

2. Who just moved into Maime Trotter's house? Who lives next door?

_____
_____ ②

3. Who is Agnes Stokes? Who is Miss Harris?

_____
_____ ②

4. What grade is Gilly in? Who is her principal?

_____
_____ ②

5. What did Gilly want more than anything else? How does she know where to reach her?

_____
_____ ②

6. How did Gilly give Miss Harris a hard time? How did Miss Harris react?

_____
_____ ②

7. What was different about William Ernest? What happened to Mr. Randolph?

_____
_____ ②

8. What did Gilly find at Mr. Randolph's on her first visit? On her second?

_____
_____ ②

9. What does Mr. Randolph do for a living? What was Mr. Randolph's prize possession?

_____
_____ ②

10. Why did Gilly write a letter filled with lies? To whom was the letter addressed?

_____
_____ ②

SUBTOTAL: /20

NAME: _____

Comprehension Quiz

40

11. What reading level was W.E. at? What did he really like to do?

_____

_____

2

12. What did Agnes do for Gilly? What did Gilly do for Agnes?

_____

_____

2

13. What did Gilly do at school that was so memorable? What is her real name?

_____

_____

2

14. Name two foster families with whom Gilly previously lived. Can you name two more?

_____

_____

2

15. What was the name of the book where Gilly found the money? What was the title of Mr. Randolph's favorite book?

_____

_____

2

16. What did Gilly master at school? What did she try to teach W.E.?

_____

_____

2

17. Who is Chadwell? What happened to him?

_____

_____

2

18. Where does Gilly end up living? Who would be proud of her?

_____

_____

2

19. What is a simile? Give two examples from the story.

_____

_____

2

20. What is a metaphor? Give two examples from the story.

_____

_____

2

SUBTOTAL: /20

The Great Gilly Hopkins CC2504

11

1. Answers will vary

2. Answers will vary

Vocabulary
1) obligingly
2) prodding
3) salvage
4) squat
5) flinch
6) bolster

12

1.
a) F
b) T
c) T
d) F
e) T
f) F

2.
a) 4
b) 3
c) 2
d) 1
e) 6
f) 5

13

1. Possible answer: She wasn't happy at all; she wanted to be with her mother

2. Answers will vary

3. Possible answer: She didn't feel like making new friends

4. Answers will vary

5. Answers will vary

6. Answers will vary

14

1. Answers will vary

2. Answers will vary

Vocabulary
1) privilege
2) curlicue
3) fanatic
4) acquaintance
5) polecat
6) lurch
7) vengeance
8) delinquency

15

1.
a) B
b) B
c) C
d) A

1.
a) A
b) C
c) A
d) C

16

1. Answers will vary

2. Answers will vary

3. Possible answer: Gilly is really a good person inside

4. Possible answer: Miss Ellis might have sweetened and sugar coated the truth

5. Possible answers:
1) Listening to that woman was like licking melted ice cream off the carton
2) Trotter's spoon went up in the air like a fly-swatter
3) … and the fat woman eating it up like hot-fudge sundae with all the nuts

EZ✓

1. Answers will vary

2. Answers will vary

3. Possible answer: Mr. Randolph can't see and cleaning must not be very important

4. Answers will vary

5. Answers will vary

(22)

1.
a) Bible
b) two five-dollar bills
c) root
d) postcard
e) encyclopedia
f) ticket

2.
a) 2
b) 6
c) 4
d) 3
e) 5
f) 1

(21)

---

1. Answers will vary; gives her confidence

2. Answers will vary

Vocabulary
Sentences will vary

(20)

---

1. Possible answer: She's afraid she'll become attached and then get hurt again

2. Answers will vary

3. a) Gilly needed to prove to everyone that she wouldn't allow herself to be stepped on; Answers will vary

a) Answers will vary

4. Possible answers:
1) That ignorant hippopotamus!

2) She would show that lard can a thing or two

(19)

1.
a) F
b) F
c) T
d) T
e) F
f) T

2. Answers will vary

(18)

---

1. Answers will vary

2. Answers will vary

Vocabulary
1) snarled, vicious

2) imbecile

3) fracas

4) favoritism

5) palsy

6) clamor

7) obscene

8) sassy

(17)

1.
Gilly stretched the truth in her letter: She was going through a desperate time, Trotter was illiterate and a religious fanatic, W.E. was probably mentally retarded, Mr. Randolph was one of Trotter's weird friends. Answers will vary.

2. $39.00; Answers will vary

3. Answers will vary

4. Answers will vary

5. Answers will vary

EZ✓

(28)

1.
a) **T**
b) **F**
c) **T**
d) **F**
e) **F**
f) **F**

2.
a) Trotter
b) Mr. Randolph
c) Miss Harris
d) Mr. Randolph
e) Agnes
f) Gilly

(27)

---

1. Answers will vary

2. Answers will vary

Vocabulary
1) marrow (n.)
2) aptitude (n.)
3) courted (v.)
4) anonymous (adj.)
5) stoke (v.)
6) cajole (v.)

(26)

---

1. Answers will vary

2. Once again Trotter was kind to her

3. Answers will vary

4. Answers will vary

5. Possible answers:
squeaked
rumbling
blamety-blam
smack
chirp
Pow!

(25)

1.
a) C b) C
c) C d) B

2.
a) A b) A
c) A d) B

(24)

---

1. Answers will vary

2. Possible answers: Maybe this isn't her mom's address, but the address of a hospital, prison, army base, employment address, etc…

Vocabulary
1) final
2) distasteful
3) distant
4) proceed
5) obscure
6) misunderstand

(23)

29

1. Answers will vary

2. Answers will vary

Vocabulary

1) eternal
2) futile
3) pirouetting
4) reluctant
5) indication
6) preservation
7) exquisite
8) dignity

30

1.
a) fake
b) impatiently
c) torture
d) lecture
e) gaudiest
f) obediently

2.
a) Miss Ellis
b) Officer Rhine
c) clerk
d) Mitchell
e) Melvin
f) Trotter

31

1. Explained to the other children what adultery is; Answers will vary

2. The relationship a married person has with someone outside of his or her marriage; Answers will vary (i.e., some think that adultery won't happen if it is not talked about it)

3. After her husband, Melvin, died, Trotter kept his clothes

4. Possible answers: Afraid of being punished; afraid that she might have to change foster homes again, and she wouldn't achieve her goal of seeing Courtney

5. The children were getting to know each other and becoming friends

6. Control of someone or something by demons or the devil

32

1. Answers will vary

2. Answer will vary

Vocabulary

Sentences will vary

33

1.
a) grandmother
b) Agnes
c) W.E.
d) grandfather

2.
a) 5
b) 2
c) 1
d) 4
e) 3

3. Answer will vary

34

1.
a) Answers will vary
b) Answers will vary
c) Possible answer: Trotter was ill, and maybe Gilly did not want to upset her at this time
d) Possible answer: Trotter was always nice to Gilly and Gilly was worried about being heartbroken again
e) Answers will vary

1. Answers will vary

2. Answers will vary

3. Answers will vary

4. Answers will vary (i.e. Both could be quiet and uneasy; Trotter's – more emotional and sad, Nonnie's – once the ice was broken, could be very revealing and informative)

5. Answers will vary

(40)

1.
- busy with horses
- worn out
- shoveling manure
- half-million-dollar prize
- have three maids
- school is terrible
- nobody knows anything
- won one race
- will skip to ninth grade

2.
a) 4
b) 2
c) 5
d) 1
e) 3
f) 7
g) 6

(39)

1. Answers will vary

2. Answers will vary

Vocabulary
1) reckon
2) anxiety
3) chatter
4) willow
5) permanent
6) gutsy
7) agony
8) sneer

(38)

1. Answers will vary

2. He died in the war

3. Answers will vary

4. Answers will vary

5. Possible answer: Chapter 12: *To stop being a "foster child", the quotation marks dragging the phrase down, almost drowning it*

(37)

1.
a) F
b) T
c) T
d) T
e) F
f) F

2.
a) W.E.
b) Mr. Randolph
c) W.E.
d) Trotter
e) Gilly
f) Grandmother

(36)

1. Answers will vary

2. Answers will vary

Vocabulary
1) kaleidoscopic
2) monogrammed
3) woefully
4) eyeing
5) expanse
6) smother

(35)

Word Search Answers

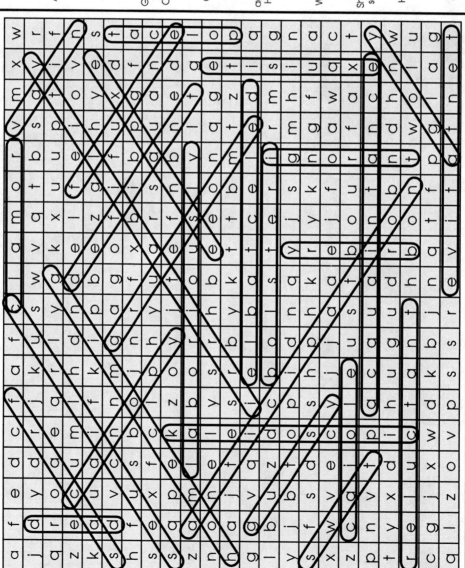

1. Trotter family: Maime Trotter, William Ernest Teague, Galadriel Hopkins Hopkins family: Galadriel Hopkins, Courtney Rutherford Hopkins, Nonnie, grandfather and Chadwell (both deceased)

2. Gilly was placed into Trotter's home. Mr. Randolph lives next door.

3. Agnes Stoke is girl at school who follows Gilly everywhere. Miss Harris is the grade six teacher.

4. Gilly is in sixth grade. Mr. Evans is her principal.

5. Gilly wanted to be with her mother Courtney Rutherford Hopkins. Courtney sent her a postcard and her address was on it.

6. Gilly made a card for Miss Harris with the message, "Black is Beautiful", but she wrote the message in very tiny letters believing that few people actually thought this was true. Miss Harris got a lot of anger out, and then she thanked Gilly for allowing her to vent.

7. William Ernest is a slow learner. Mr. Randolph is blind.

8. She found 2 five-dollar bills. On the second visit she found 34 dollars.

9. He is retired. His book collection, especially The Oxford Book of English Verse.

10. Gilly was very miserable. It was addressed to Courtney (her mom).

11. He could read at the Orange level. W.E. loved to watch television.

12. Agnes became Gilly's friend. Gilly became Agnes' friend (but not her best friend).

13. Gilly fought with six boys at recess. Her real name is Galadriel Hopkins.

14. The Nixons, Richmonds, Nevins, Newmans, and Trotters.

15. Gilly found the money in Sarsaparilla to Sorcery. Mr. Randolph's favorite book was The Oxford Book of English Verse.

16. Gilly mastered the metric system. She taught W.E. how to defend himself with his mouth and his fists.

17. Chadwell is Nonnie's son (Courtney's brother). He died during the Vietnam war.

18. Gilly ends up living with Nonnie. Trotter would be proud of her.

19. A simile is a comparison of two different things, often using the word like or as. Examples will vary.

20. A metaphor is comparison of two things in which one thing is described as being something completely unrelated. Examples will vary.